Dealing With the December Dilemma

December Lessons for the 21st Century

By Elizabeth Chapin-Pinotti

Table of Contents

#1   Countering the December Dilemma

Photos for Brainstorm – Fourth of July

#3   Miwok Big Time

#4   Student Page: Indian Grinding Rock

#5   Photo for Indian Grinding Rock Activity

#6   Student Page: Chaw'se

#7   Student Page: Miwok Roundhouse

#8   Hanukkah

#9   Student Page: The Dreidel

#10   Student Page: Make a Dreidel

#11   Ramadan

#12   Student Page: Ramadan

#13   Student Page: Good Deed Quilt

#14   Kwanzaa

#15   Student Page: Kwanzaa

#16:   Christmas

#17   Student Page: The Origin of the Christmas Tree

#18   Student Page: My Christmas Tree Origin Story

#19:   Student Page: Traditions I Do

#20   Student Page: My Traditions Comic Strip

#21   Holiday RAFT Assignment

#22   What is a R.A.F.T.?

#23   RAFT Rubric

#24   My Investigation

#25   Holiday Cutouts for My Investigation

#26   Holiday Cutouts for My Investigation

#27   Kwanmisadomakuh Big Time: Literature Unit

            Original Illustrated Story

            Common Core Aligned Literature Study Worksheets

Visit My TPT Store: https://www.teacherspayteachers.com/Store/Elizabeths-Lessons

My Pinterest: https://www.pinterest.com/epinotti/

My Facebook: https://www.facebook.com/ReadingAllAround/

Borders: https://www.teacherspayteachers.com/Store/Krista-Wallden

Countering the December Dilemma

This lesson provides opportunities for students to learn about holidays and celebrations practiced by different countries and cultural groups in the United States and round the world.

Goal: The goal of this lesson is for students to explore different holiday and celebrations and gain insight into cultural values, beliefs and history of diverse groups.

Objectives:
- Students will learn about Hanukkah
- Students will learn about Miwok Big Time
- Students will learn about Ramadan
- Students will learn about Kwanzaa
- Students will learn about Christmas
- Students will identify characteristics that holidays have in common
- Students will discover differences in the ways holidays are celebrated
- Students will research holidays and celebrations observed in the United States
- Students will present their research to the class.

Brainstorm:

On the board or Smartboard, braintorm holidays and celebrations your class celebrates with their families

Explain to students they will learn about some of the holidays and celebrations observed by different cultures. Show students the picture on the following page of the U.S. Fourth of July celebration. Ask students to think about, and discuss in pairs, the following: If people in other countries say these pictures would they get an accurate picture of everyday life in the United States?

Ask: Why or why not?
Have students report out their answers.

At the end of the discussion, tell students that they are going to learn about holidays and celebrations and that what they are learning doesn't necessarily reflect everyday life. Explain how pictures and information in isolation gives us insight into what other people believe but doesn't necessary give us a window into their everyday worlds.

Fourth of July

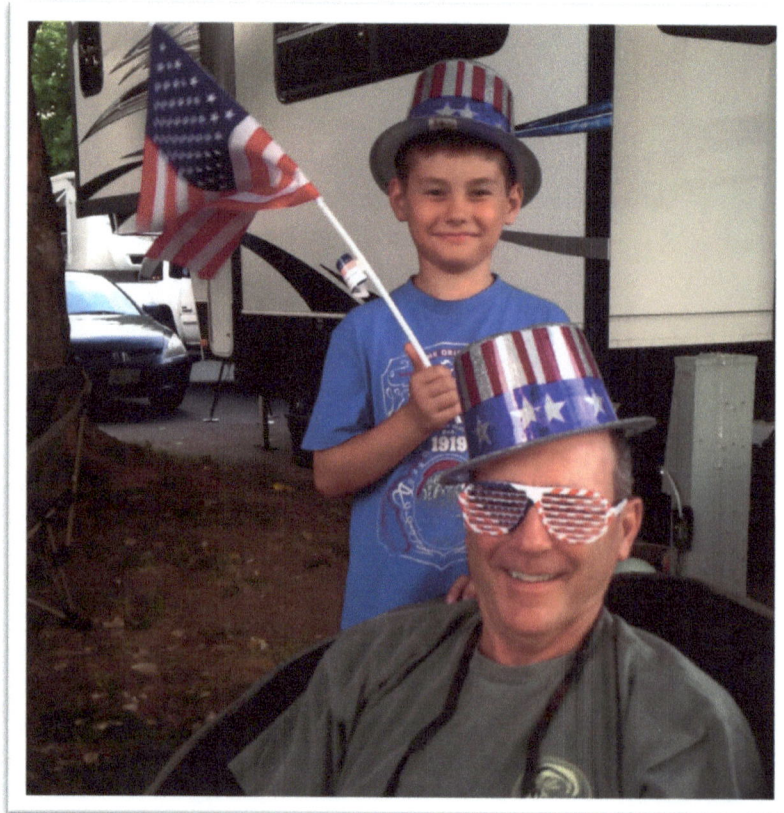

Miwok Big Time
Acorn Festival

Background: The Miwok Indians of Northern California, relied on acorns harvested from valley oaks as a major food source. They picked the acorns in the fall and stored them in cha'ka or granaries. The acorns could not be eaten as picked, but rather had to be "processed" to get rid of the tannin, which prevents the body from absorbing the nutrients in the acorns. Tannins also give acorns their bitter taste.

To process acorns, the nut is cracked open and the meat inside is ground to a meal, like corn meal. This was done with stone pestles in mortar holes formed on large slabs of rocks. The California foothills are dotted with such holes in stone. The largest slabs of marbleized limestone, called chaw'se or grinding rocks, can be found near Volcano, California at the California Indian Grinding Rock State Park. There are more than 1,000 holes at Chaw'se and are a sight to see.

After the acorn meat was make into meal, it was rinsed over and over again to wash away the tannin. Then it was used to make soup, mush or acorn bread. Acorns are very high in nutritional value and the average Miwok adult eat about 2,000 pounds of them per year.

The Acorn Festival, or Big Time, is a gathering to celebrate the acorn harvest. Families from villages far and wide would come and eat and talk and exchange news and supplies. This is an ancient harvest festival, largely religious, with ceremonial rites and traditional dances.

The ceremonial dances are performed in roundhouses – like the one at Grinding Rock State Park. The roundhouse there is the largest around: at 60 feet in diameter, it is supported by cedar poles and has a cedar bark slab roof. The Miwok Big Time is held on the fourth weekend in September.

Information from: http://www.brownielocks.com/miwok.html

Teaching Note: For the printable "Indian Grinding Rock #1 – project the picture on the next page on the board. It is from Indian Grinding Rock State Park.

Miwok Big Time in the Classroom

1. Miwok information:
   http://what-when-how.com/native-americans/miwok-native-americans-of-california/
2. http://www.chawseassociation.org/the-rock.html

Indian Grinding Rock

That big limestone grinding rock below is located at Grinding Rock State Park in California and has become a monument to the Miwok survival. It has almost 1,200 grinding or mortar holes -- more than any other grinding rock in North America!

This stone is also distinguishable and remarkable because it has 363 petroglyphs that depict circles, wavy lines and human and tracks.

It is believed that these petroglyphs are approximately 2,000 to 3,000 years old. They tell the story of the history of the Miwok in the lower California foothills. Except for one other smaller stone at another site, the stone at the Grinding Rock State Park is one of two that are etched with such petroglyphs.

Every year, on the fourth weekend in September, Miwoks gather at Grinding Rock for the Big Time Acorn Festival. The festival is a gathering to celebrate the acorn harvest. Families still come from far and wide to eat and talk and exchange news. This is still considered an ancient harvest festival, largely religious, with ceremonial rites and traditional dances.

Think and Write

What are the "Grinding Rocks": _____

_____

_____

_____

Why is Big Time Important: _____

_____

_____

_____

_____

_____

_____

Chaw'se from Indian Grinding Rock State Park California

This Grinding Rock Belongs to the Northern Sierra Miwok

Name: _____

Chaw'se

Chaw'se is pronounced Cha-sa. It is the Miwok work for "mortar" cup. For thousands and thousands of years, the Northern Sierra Miwok lived on the land that is now Indian Grinding Rock State Park in California and cherished the landscape. Not only is Grinding Rock home to Miwok ancestors, but part of the thriving native community today.

Chaw'se is a spiritual place of gathering place where traditions, rich culture and dance thrive.

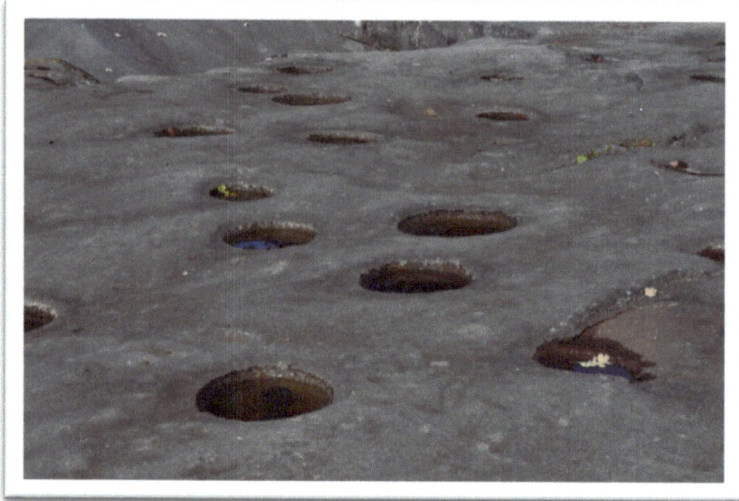

The grinding rock is the largest in North America and it is much more than a stone, for in the Miwok culture, the rock is viewed as a living thing.

It embodies the years of seasons that have passed. It has also felt the slow shaping of the mortars, by women's hands, for over a thousand years.

Think and Write

Think about what it would have been like to gather and grind acorns. Describe how you think a typical gathering and grinding day would go. Be sure to use lots of detail.

_____

_____

_____

_____

_____

_____

_____

_____

_____

Name: _____

Miwok Roundhouse

A roundhouse was the center of the community for the Miwok. Only a tribal headsman was given the responsibility of building the roundhouse, or hun'ge, for the village. The roundhouse was and is a very sacred places with much spiritual significance.

This roundhouse stands as a powerful symbol of survival for the Northern Sierra Miwoks. Despite the loss of life and land – the Miwok continue to dance in this hun'ge and follow traditions established by their ancestors.

Think and Write

What is the center of your community? _____

_____

What traditions do you celebrate with your family or community? _____

_____

_____

_____

_____

_____

_____

Hanukkah

Background: Hanukkah is celebrated by Jewish people around the same time Christians celebrate Christmas. Hanukkah reflects on the victory of the Maccabees or Israelites over the Greek-Syrian ruler, Antiochus about 2200 years ago. It all began when this ruler told everyone they had to warship the Greek gods. He took over the Temple of Jerusalem and took down all of the Jewish holy symbols.

Antiochus's actions led to a revolt. It took two years, but finally the revolt was successful. The Temple was liberated and rededicated. The Temple was cleansed, a new altar was set and new holy vessels were made. According to the Talmud, pure olive oil with the seal of the kohen gadol (high priest) was needed for the menorah in the Temple, which was required to burn throughout the night every night. The story goes that one flask of oil was found – which was only enough to burn for one day, only it burned for eight days, the time it took to prepare a fresh supply of kosher oil for the menorah. An eight-day festival was declared to commemorate this miracle.

FUN FACTS:

A Menorah is a special nine-branched candelabrum.

Each night of Hanukkah, an additional candle is placed in the Menorah from right to left, and then lit from left to right. On the last night, all the candles are lit.

A dreidel is a four-sided top that has a Hebrew letter on each side.

During Hanukkah, families eat foods fried in oil, such as latkes (potato pancakes) and sufganiot (jelly donuts) to remember the miracle of the Festival of Lights.

Traditionally, Hanukkah is a time when children are encouraged and rewarded for their Torah studies. This led to giving children Hanukkah money and presents during the holiday.

During the eight days of Hanukkah, the entire Hallel (psalms of praise) is said.

Except during times of religious persecution, the menorah was placed outside the front door. Today the menorah shines in the window of every Jewish home.

Savings bonds, checks, and small chocolate coins wrapped in gold foil-these are the modern incarnations of the traditional gift known as Hanukkah gelt. "Gelt" is a Yiddish term for "money".

Hanukkah is celebrated in the home beginning on the 25th day of the Jewish month of Kislev.

Hanukkah in the Classroom

1. Introduce Hanukkah to students and then show *The Story of Hanukkah*: https://www.youtube.com/watch?v=7tws_uMAEOs
2. PBSkids http://pbskids.org/video/?guid=20e21806-5ddb-4c2c-9d34-86036a9a0f3f
3. Partner up students and have them read "The Dreidel" and answer the questions
4. Make dreidels
5. Play the dreidel game. It is fun to have chocolate coins on hand to play with

The Dreidel

The dreidel is played with by Jewish children during Hanukkah. It looks like a top, but it is so much more.

When the Syrians forbid study of the Torah, or Jewish Written Law, Jews studied it anyway – only if anyone approached, they would pull out their tops and pretend to be playing.

Outside of Israel, a dreidel has the Hebrew letters "nun," "gimel," "hay," and "shin" on its four sides. These letters stand for "Nes gadol haya sham," which means:

"A great miracle happened there,"

A dreidel in Israel has the letter "pay" instead of "shin" on it This stands for "poh," meaning "here" – "a great miracle happened here."

The Hebrew letters also represent Yiddish words that tell how to play the dreidel game. Each player begins with the same amount of candies, chocolate coins (gelt), or other tokens, and puts one in a pot. Players take turns spinning the dreidel, waiting to see which letter lands face up. Nun is for "nisht," nothing – do nothing. Gimel is for "gants," whole – take the whole pot. Hay is for "halb," half – take half. Shin is for "shtel," to put in – add to the pot. The game ends when a single player wins all of the candy or gelt.

Explain how to play the dreidel game:

_____

_____

_____

_____

_____

_____

_____

_____

_____

_____

_____

_____

Tell why the dreidel is important

_____

_____

_____

_____

_____

_____

_____

Make a dreidel
and play the
dreidel game
with your friends

Nun נ
Gimel ג
Hei ה
Shin ש

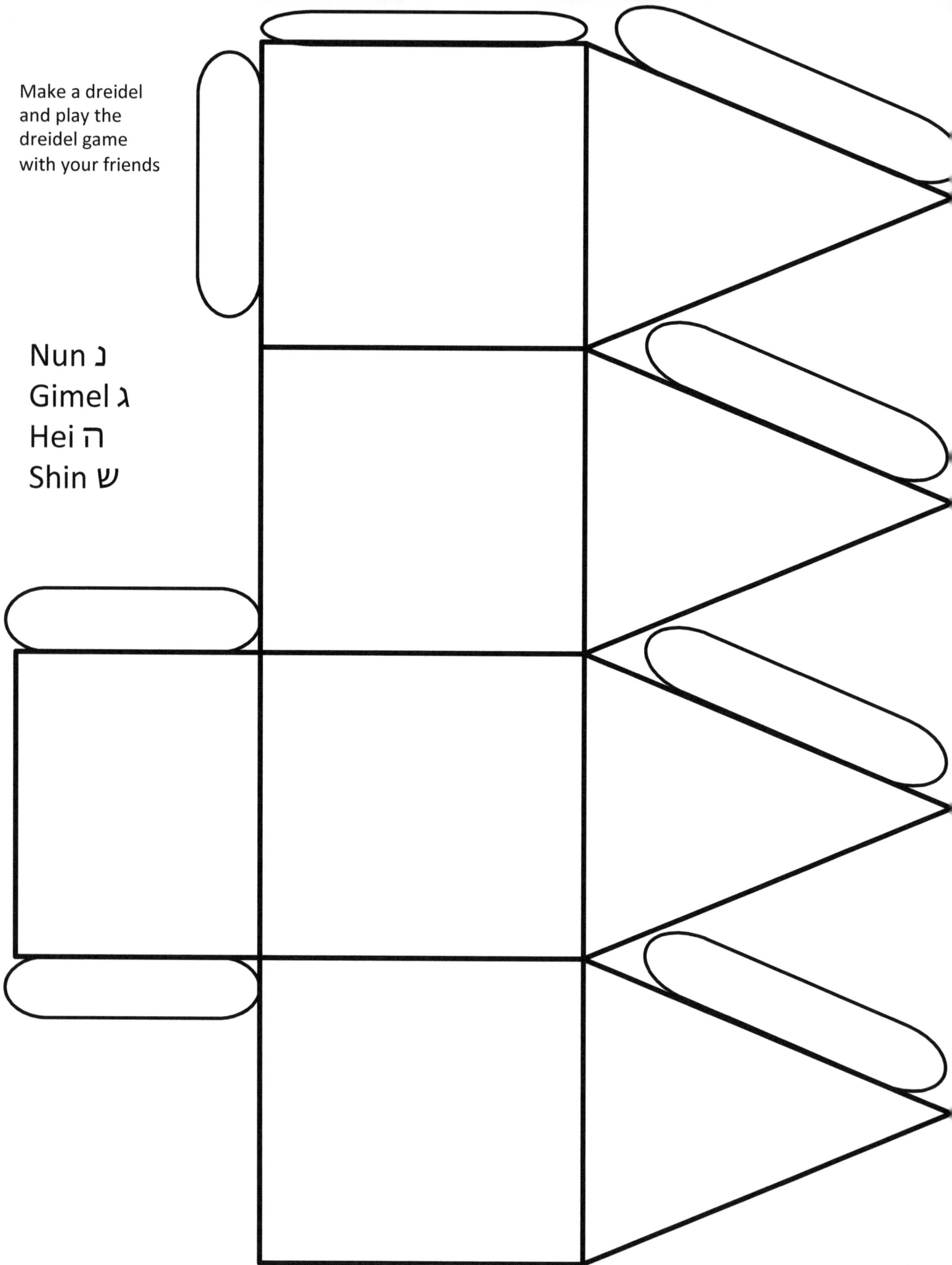

Ramadan

Introduce Ramadan and share one or both of these videos with your class:

https://www.youtube.com/watch?v=SVNe5DyOFK8
https://www.youtube.com/watch?v=7kM27b-iaBg

Background: The ninth month of the Muslim calendar is Ramadan. It is a very holy month for Muslims, because it is the month in which the Quran was first revealed. The Quran is the divine book of guidance for Muslims as they believe that God, Allah in Arabic, revealed it to the prophet Muhammad through the angel Gabriel. The entire revelation took 23 years.

During Ramadan, everyone over twelve-years-old fasts from dawn until dusk. They do not eat or drink anything – including water. They try very hard to be good, do good deeds and do nothing bad.

On the 27th day of the month of Ramadan, Muslims celebrate the Night of Power. In Arabic, the Night of Power is translated as Al-Qadr. This is a very holy night as it is the night when Allah delivered the Quran to Muhammad. The Quran says, it is on this night that Allah determines the course of the world for the next year.

Ramadan ends with the feast of Eid-Ul-Fitr. Friends and families gather for large meals and to just be together.

Ramadan in the Classroom

Good Deed Quilt:

Using colored pens, pencils or crayons have students write a list of things that they plan do to help their family, friends or people around the world. For example, carry in groceries, pick up cans or read to the young or old, place them on their triangles and decorate their quilts. Post the quilts in your classroom and have students check off good deeds they have accomplished.

Ramadan Classroom ideas:
http://www.scholastic.com/teachers/article/celebrating-cultural-diversity-ramadan-1

Ramadan

The ninth month of the Muslim calendar is Ramadan. It is a very holy month, because it is the month in which the Quran was first revealed. The Quran is the divine book of guidance. Muslims believe that God, Allah in Arabic, revealed it to the prophet Muhammad through the angel Gabriel. The entire revelation took 23 years.

During Ramadan, everyone over twelve-years-old fasts from dawn until dusk. They do not eat or drink anything – including water. They try very hard to be good, do good deeds and do nothing bad.

On the 27th day of the month of Ramadan, Muslims celebrate the Night of Power. In Arabic, the Night of Power is translated as Al-Qadr. This is a very holy night as it is the night when Allah delivered the Quran to Muhammad. The Quran says, it is on this night that Allah determines the course of the world for the next year.

Ramadan ends with the feast of Eid-Ul-Fitr. Friends and families gather for large meals and to just be together.

List five facts about Ramadan:

1. _____

2. _____

3. _____

4. _____

5. _____

Good Deed Quilt by

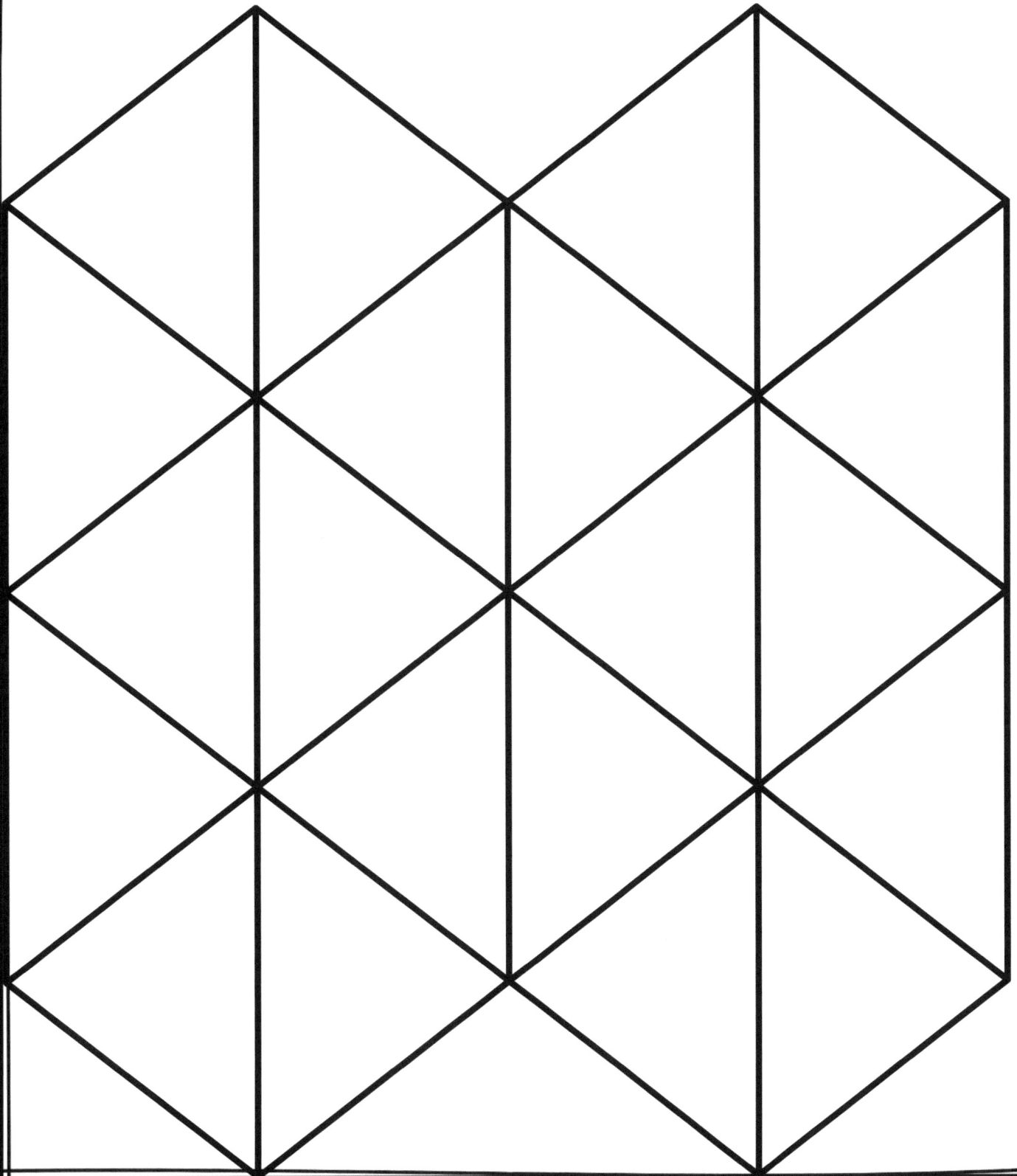

_____

Kwanzaa

Introduce Kwanzaa and show:

- Seven Principles of Kwanzaa Video:
  https://www.youtube.com/watch?v=o_frs4KQ_aE
- Have students sing and clap along with:
  https://www.youtube.com/watch?v=kS9d9eGAo2g

Kwanzaa is not a religious or a political holiday. *Kwanzaa is a reflective holiday,* introduced in the mid-1960's in the U.S. during the Civil Rights Movement. It is a time when African-Americans celebrate their African heritage.

Kwanzaa begins each year on December 26 and lasts through the first day in January. The symbols of Kwanzaa are African harvest symbols, like ears of dried corn and colorfully woven tablecloths. People decorate their homes for Kwanzaa.

An important symbol is the wooden candlestick. This candlestick holds 7 candles in a row. The center candle is black, to signify unity. There are 3 red candles on one side, and 3 green candles on the other.

Each of the candles stands for one of the 7 Principles of Kwanzaa:

1. umoja - to maintain unity in the family and community
2. kujichagulia - self-determination, to be responsible and speak for oneself
3. ujima - collective work and responsibility, to build and maintain a community
4. ujamaa - economic co-operation, to help and profit one another
5. nia - purpose, to build and develop the community for the benefit of the people
6. kuumba - creativity, to do everything possible to leave the community more beautiful and beneficial for future generations
7. imani - faith, to believe in parents, teachers and leaders.

Corn is another symbol of Kwanzaa. One ear of corn is placed under the kinara to symbolize each child in a family.

Karamu: the Kwanzaa Feast: On the sixth day of Kwanzaa a feast is held. The sixth day of Kwanzaa falls on December 31. December 31 is the day that honors creativity so many families organize a craft making party. The gift giving day is January 1 – and the crafts are often the gifts given.

Kwanzaa in the Classroom

A modern take on the old gift exchange is a craft party and classroom gift exchange – or a craft party and a gift giving to younger students.

Kwanzaa Craft Ideas: http://www.activityvillage.co.uk/kwanzaa-crafts

Kwanzaa

Each day of Kwanzaa is dedicated to one of seven ideas or principles|

Day 1: Unity	**How will you strive to maintain Unity in your family and community?**
	_____
	_____
	_____
Day 2: Self-determination	How do you make sure you speak and create for yourself?
	_____
	_____
	_____
	_____
Day 3: Collective Work and Responsibility	How do you work with others to solve problems?
	_____
	_____
Day 4: Collective Economics	How will you work together to make sure everyone has enough money?
	_____
	_____
	_____
Day 5: Purpose	How will you help to make your community strong?
	_____
	_____
	_____
Day 6: Creativity	How can you make your community more beautiful for the next generation?
	_____
	_____
	_____
Day 7: Faith	How do you show that you believe in your people with all of your heart?
	_____
	_____

Christmas

Background: Christmas is celebrated on December 25 by Christians around the world. The celebration usually beings on December 24: Christmas Eve. The Christmas holiday celebrates the birth of Christ.

Christmas is the observance of Jesus' humble birth to to Mary in a stable in Bethlehem. The holiday also celebrates the angel's appearance to shepherds, telling them to visit the newborn king. Christians believe that Jesus is the son of God who was born to save them from sin.

Christians believe that the true meaning of Christmas is love. God loved His own and provided a way—the only Way—for us to spend eternity with Him. He gave His only Son to take our punishment for our sins. He paid the price in full, and we are free from condemnation when we accept that free gift of love.

Symbols of Christmas:

- Santa Claus: Santa Claus symbolizes giving
- Candy Canes: The candy cane is the shape of a shepherd's crook – reminding Christians that Jesus, who is also known as the good shepherd came into the world.
- Wreaths: Wreaths are traditionally made from evergreens and are shaped in a circle to show no beginning and no end to love.
- Star: Christians believe that the star led the wise men to Jesus.

Christmas in the Classroom

Watch
- What is Christmas About: Clip from Charlie Brown Christmas Special: https://www.youtube.com/watch?v=pn10FF-FQfs
- Christmas Around the World: https://www.youtube.com/watch?v=LwN_Kcb-XhM

Do:
http://www.allfreekidscrafts.com/Kids-Christmas-Crafts/Christmas-Craft-Ideas-for-the-Classroom

The Origin of the Christmas Tree

One Story: Many pagan cultures worshipped evergreens. They were believed to be symbols of immortality – meaning that one could live forever. They also used them to ward off evil spirits. In the early 700's, Saint Boniface, who converted the German people to Christianity, clear cut the Oak of Thor, the mighty sacred tree worshipped by the Saxons. From its roots grew a fir tree which Boniface took as a sign of the Christian faith.

Another Story: In early 1500, Martin Luther brought a small tree indoors and decorated it with candles in honor of Christ's birth. This practice took off and was a tradition by the 18th century and become the custom in France, Germany, and Austria.

Last One: The Christmas tree represents the original Tree of Paradise, the burning bush which spoke to Moses, the branch of Jesse from which Jesus was born, the life-giving tree of the cross of Christ, and the tree which St. John the Apostle saw in the Book of Revelations whose leaves have medicine for the people and which yields fruit each month for the healing of the nations. Because it is green year-round, the evergreen tree represents hope. Its needles and its narrow crest point upward, turning our thoughts to heaven. Because the tree is cut down and then erected again, it is a symbol of Christ's resurrection.

Which story of the origin of the Christmas tree do you like best and why? _____
_____
_____
_____
_____
_____

Name: _____ Date: _____

My Christmas Tree Origin Story

Directions: Write your own story about how you think the Christmas tree became a holiday tradition. Be sure to be creative.

Traditions

A **tradition** is a belief or behavior passed down within a group or society with symbolic meaning or special significance with origins in the past.

What are some traditions you and your family or community practice? Please be specific and use detail:

_____

_____

_____

_____

_____

_____

_____

_____

_____

_____

_____

_____

_____

_____

Traditions

Make up a comic strip about your traditions.

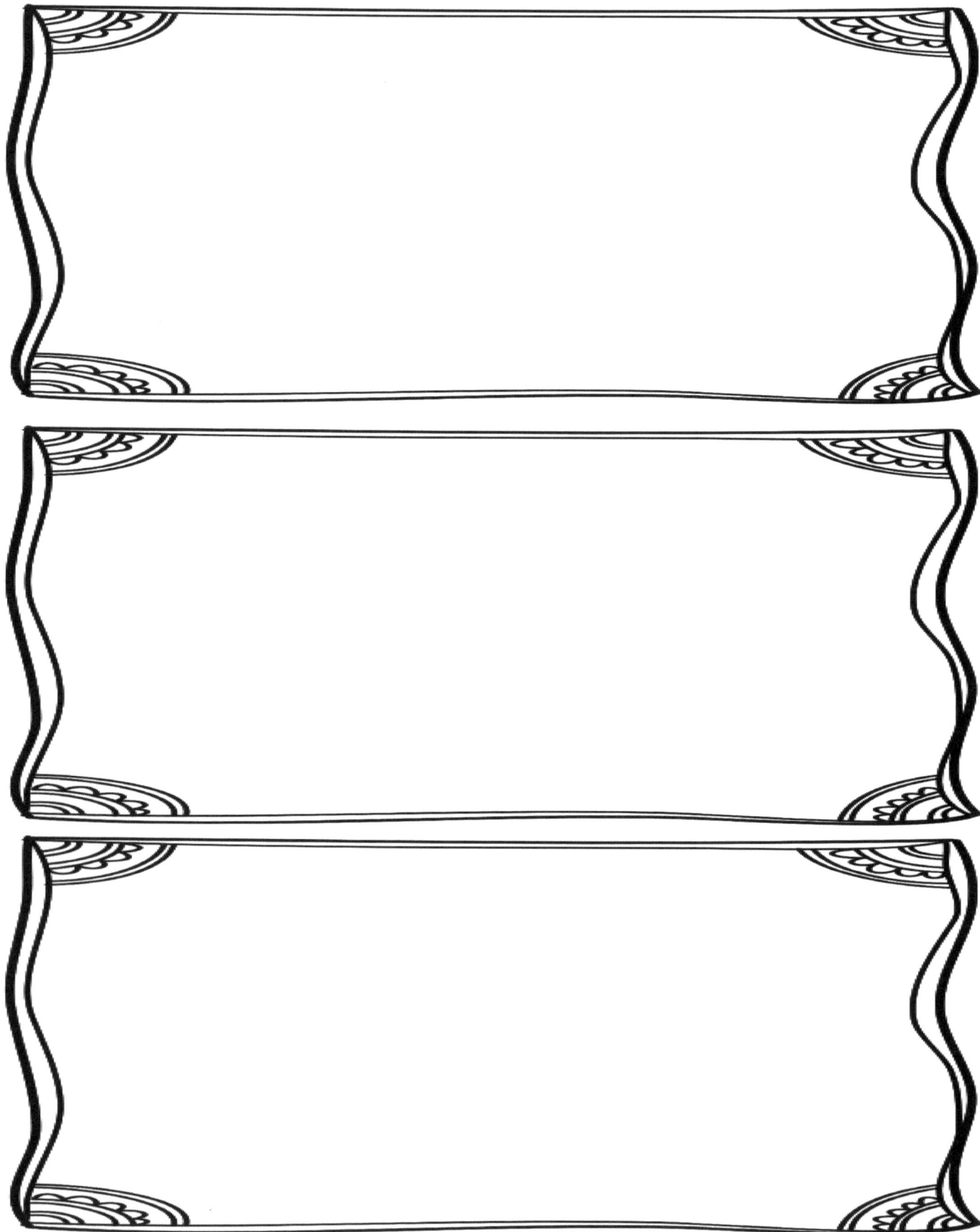

Holiday RAFT

Have a whole group discussion on the following after each lesson:

•What did you learn about the _____culture from learning about _____? Choose a culture: Miwok, Muslim, Jewish, African-American, Christmas

•Why did the holiday begin?

•What are some other holidays you know about?

•What are symbols used in...name the holiday you studied.

•What are symbols in other holidays you know?

•What are some similarities in the holidays we've talked about? In others?

•Some common themes: harvest, people, religion, historical events, new year, spring, freedom, independence, culture

Research Project: Explain to students they are going to research holidays celebrated around the world. Explain that the holidays are celebrated in the United States, but many have their origins in other countries.

Put specific holidays and celebrations in a box for students to randomly choose.

Divide students into pairs or threes and have each pairing or threesome choose a holiday. Explain to students they are going to use the internet or the library – Chromebook labs or computer lab – whatever you have available. If necessary – print research from the internet and have on hand for students. The ideal situation is to have students do internet research.

Tell students they will use their research to do a RAFT project and then present it to the class.

Pass out the handout: **My Investigation**

What is R.A.F.T.?

Raft is a strategy for providing different options for students to demonstrate their learning. R.A.F.T. is the 1982 brainchild of Dorothy Vandevander and is a great way for students of varying levels to transform content knowledge in engaging and fun ways – as R.A.F.T. allows students to choose the means by which they communicate their knowledge of information learned. R.A.F.T. assignments allow students to discover their own voices and formations for presenting content information.

The benefits of a R.A.F.T. assignment are numerous. Students are asked to display knowledge from a real world perspective and, because they are considering perspective as they go through the writing process, they think more critically and work at a much higher level than when they merely apply the essay writing process.

R.A.F.T.

R	Role	Students decide their role. They identify their role as the writer or conveyer of information for the task
A	Audience	To whom does the writer speak? What is the audience?
F	Format	What form will a student's response take? How will they demonstrate they've learned the content knowledge at hand?
T	Topic	What is the topic? Ask students to think of the best way to communicate critical information of their topic?

Possible R.A.F.T. assignments for *Go Set a Watchman* pre-reading assignment:

Role	Audience	Format	Topic
Newspaper Reporter	Readers in the 1950s	Obituary	Holiday or Celebration
Attorney	US Supreme Court	Appeal Speech	Holiday or Celebration
Talk Show Host	Television	Talk Show	Holiday or Celebration
Advertiser	Magazine Audience	Print Ad	Holiday or Celebration
Fiction Writer for Children	School children today	Storybook	Holiday or Celebration
Yearbook Editor	High School Students	Yearbook Entries	Holiday or Celebration

Raft Rubric			
	4 Mastery	3 Well Done	2. Needs Word	1 Not Yet
Role: How authentic were you in portraying your role? Were you convincing?				
Audience: How well did you address audience's needs? Did you convey the content knowledge in a way that was under-standable and engaging to your audience?				
Format: How successful where you in demon-strating your understanding of the content knowledge in the chosen format?				
Topic: How well did your writing demonstrate mastery of the content?				
Conventions: Was your writing, grammar and spelling up to the task.				
Other:				

My Investigation

Questions to consider when completing your RAFT

1. Where did your holiday or celebration begin?

2. How did your holiday begin?

3. What is the point or purpose of your holiday?

4. From what part of the world did your holiday originate?

5. In what countries is your holiday celebrated today?

6. In what parts of the United States is your holiday celebrated?

7. Who celebrates your holiday? (the citizens of France, Canadians, Jews, Christians...)

8. On what date or when is your holiday celebrated?

9. How long does the celebration last?

10. If it is religious, how is it religious?

11. Are there any foods or fasting associated with your holiday? What are they? Why are they significant?

12. What are the symbols of the holidays?

13. Are there gift giving traditions associated with the holiday?

14. What do people wear on your holiday? Traditional vs. modern if different.

15. What do you think this holiday reveals about the people who celebrate it?

4th of July	Big Time Miwok Harvest Festival
Chinese New Year	Cinco de Mayo
Easter	Juneteenth
Naw Ruz	Passover
Sukkot	St. Patrick's Day
Thanksgiving	Yom Kippur
Labor Day	St. Lucia Day
Basanth	Holi
Songkran	Aboakyere

Arapaho Sun Dance	Australia Day
Bastille Day	Thanksgiving
Marti Gras	Veteran's Day
Memorial Day	Diwali
Las Posadas	Iroquois Midsummer Ceremony
Hopi Powamu Festival	Apache Girls' Sunrise Ceremony
Navajo Night Chant Ceremony	Shalako Ceremony
Bonfire Night	St. Andrew's Day

Kwanmisadomakuh Big Time! Literature Unit

This literature unit contains an original story, illustrations for students to color and Common Core State Standards-Aligned activities.

Pass it out to students and have them partner read or work alone. It is also a great story for students to practice and read to younger buddy students as the message is inclusion and helps foster cultural competence.

#1 : Comprehension Quiz c,b,a,d,b,b,a

#2: Problem Solution Interactive Notebook Page RL.5

#3: About Kwanmisadomakuh RL.1 and 2

#4: Summarize Kwanmisadomakuh RL.2

#5: Summarize RL.1

#6: Story Motivation and Evidence RL.5

#7: Stop and Think Critical Thinking Questions

#8: Possible Critical Thinking #7 Answers

Kwanmisadomakuh Big Time!

1

Kwanmisadomakuh Big Time!

Janie jumped out of bed, looked at her clock and screamed! "December 1! Merry Christmas everyone!"

In her house Christmas did not begin until December 1. No combo Christmas tree and school clothes shopping for the Tuckers.

She got dressed and ran to the kitchen with visions of sugarplums dancing in her head.

"Morning Janie," her mother said brightly.

"Mom, what's a sugarplum? They're dancing all around my head and I have no idea what they're supposed to look like," Janie said, matter-of-factly as she gulped the milk her mother put in front of her.

Mom smiled. "It's hard candy. Usually round and purple."

"My brain knew that," Janie exclaimed. "That's exactly what was dancing."

She gobbled her oatmeal. "I love today!" she said with a mouthful. "Today we get to decorate the classroom and start singing Christmas carols."

Her mother approached the table and sat directly across from her. Janie put down her milk. When Mom sat directly across and put on her serious face – it was never good.

"Janie you go to public school now," Mom said. "It's not like St. Anne's. Not everybody celebrates Christmas. I doubt you will be decorating or singing."

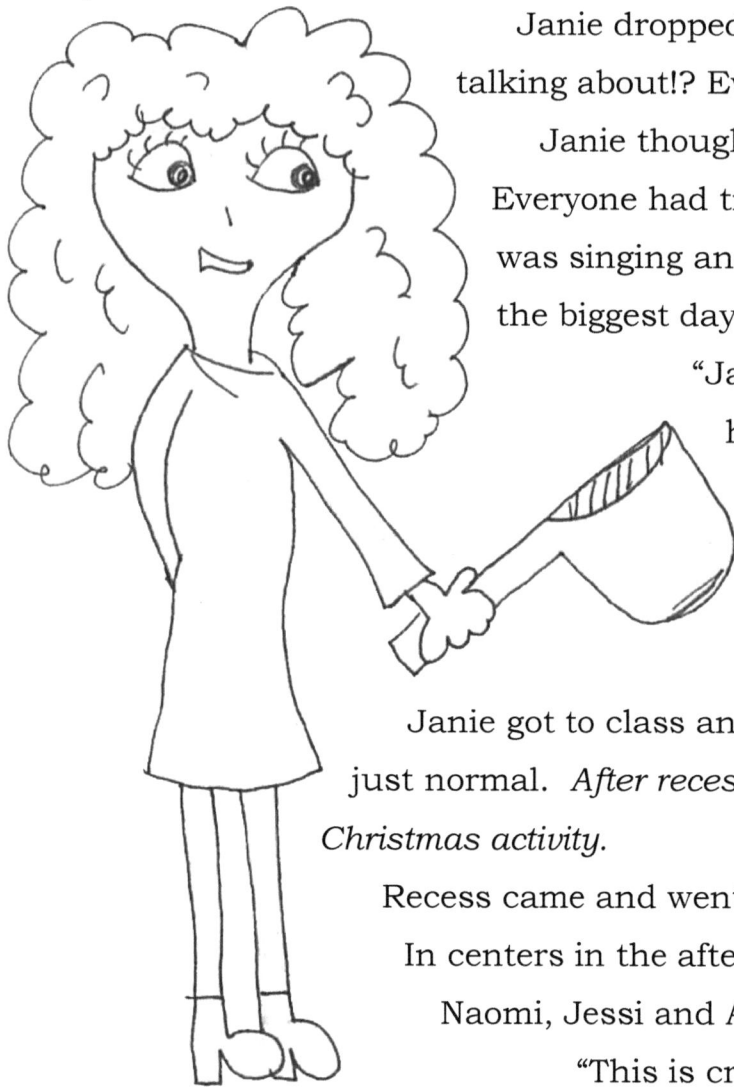

Janie dropped her spoon. "What in the world are you talking about!? Everybody celebrates Christmas."

Janie thought about all of her friends and family. Everyone had trees and celebrated the birth of Jesus. There was singing and holiday food and everything. It is one of the biggest days of the year. Her mother must be wrong.

"Janie..." her mother began, but then the bus horn sounded and Janie sprang for the door.

"See you," she grabbed her backpack, kissed her mom and hopped on the bus just in time.

Janie got to class and the day was normal – which wasn't bad – just normal. *After recess,* she thought, *that's when we'll do our first Christmas activity.*

Recess came and went and so did lunch – still nothing.

In centers in the afternoon, Janie was cooperatively working with Naomi, Jessi and Aadab.

"This is crazy!" Janie said in her quiet voice.

"What's crazy?" Naomi asked, cutting pocket out of paper for her interactive notebook.

"That we aren't starting our Christmas stuff. There's two and a half weeks until vacation. We won't have time to do our Christmas show or anything," Janie answered.

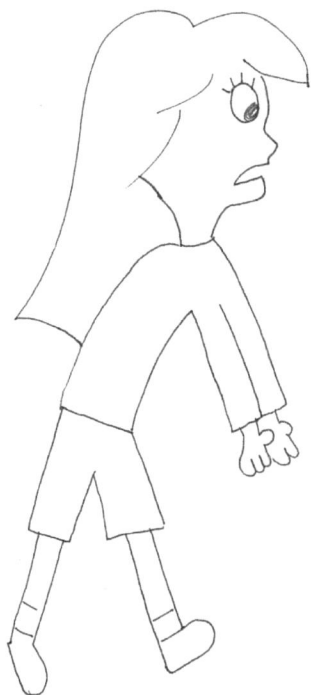

"We don't do that here," said Aadab.

"What!" Janie exclaimed. *Was mom right?* she thought.

"Oh yeah," said Jessi, "you went to Catholic school. Some of us don't even celebrate Christmas."

A rush of feelings overtook Janie. She was sad and confused and angry her parents would put her in a school that deprived her of Christmas.

After dinner that night she told her parents how bad school had been and how sad she was to miss out on Christmas when all of her friends at St. Anne's still got to celebrate.

"We'll celebrate here, Janie," Dad said. "We're going to Nonnie and Nono's farm this weekend to get our tree."

"And the poinsettias are sure to be up at church on Sunday. You do like your poinsettias."

Janie sighed, "It won't be the same. I want to go back to St. Anne's with my own people."

"Janie you love your new school and you and Naomi have been 4-H friends for years," Mom said.

"Do you know she doesn't celebrate Christmas either?" Janie said.

"They're Jewish," Dad said. "In December they celebrate Hanukkah."

"And Aadab is Muslim and celebrates Ramadan," Mom added.

"Jessi is Baptist. I've worked with her mom on

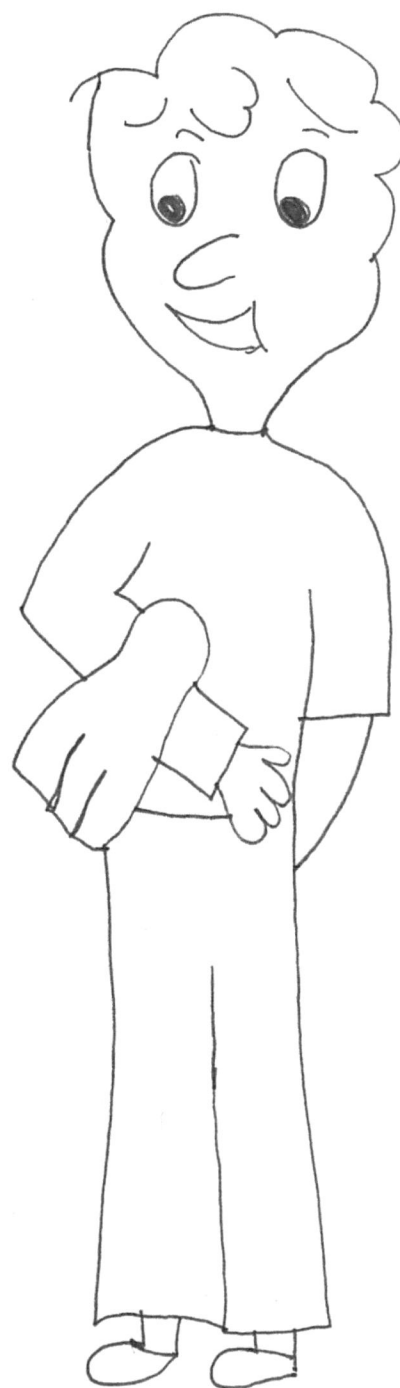

the Joint Faith Council," Mom said, "but they celebrate Kwanza too."

"This is crazy. Why don't they just celebrate Christmas like we do? Like George Washington did? Like the Pilgrims did?" Janie knew her American history and knew the United States was founded on religious freedom. "Ut-oh!"

"What?" Dad and Mom asked together.

"The Pilgrims came here to be the religion they wanted," she was beginning to understand. "That means any, not just Christians."

"You got it, Pumpkin," Dad said.

"I gotta fix this," Janie said running up the stairs and locking herself in her room.

At first recess, Janie gathered her friends.

"I get we don't all celebrate the same thing, but that doesn't mean we can't celebrate something," she said.

Naomi's eyes narrowed. "What do you mean?"

"Well, I think we should find something common in all of our different holidays and ask if we can celebrate that," Janie said.

"You just want cupcakes," Aadab laughed.

"I want the spirit of the season," Janie waved her arms in the air for emphasis. "It isn't about trees or about presents or that kind of stuff...it's about the way it feels to say Merry Christmas to someone and know by the look in their eyes they have a happy spot too. It's about knowing that at least one time during the year – peace on earth is the message. We have to have that too. We have to have a joy to the world."

"I think it is a great idea," Jessi agreed with Janie. "Tell us about Ramadan Aadab. Maybe we can find something common in what we believe."

"Ramadan is a time to think about our family and friends and doing good deeds. We only eat when it's dark. This way we can focus on other things. During Ramadan we spend more time with our families and pledge not to tell lies or to be greedy or gossip."

"Wow, those are just like Christian things," Janie said.

"The month of Ramadan is about healing and caring and hoping. It's about helping those who don't have as much as we do," Aadab finished.

"Hanukkah's about hope too," Naomi said. "In a way it was like our fight for religious freedom. A long time ago, a Syrian king ruled Judea. He said that Jews had to stop worshipping Yahweh and worship the Greek gods and then he took over the Temple of Jerusalem."

"Not very Christmasy there," Janie mumbled.

"My people fought for three years and finally got our temple back. To celebrate they lit a lamp but they didn't have a lot of oil. Only, by some miracle, the light shined for eight days. That's why we celebrate for eight days and nights. They never gave up hope and won the Temple back."

"Jesus was Jewish," Janie said. "I just automatically thought that would mean Jewish people believed what I believe."

"I think Jesus was the son of God," Jessi smiled at Naomi, "but I also celebrate Kwanza.

Kwanzaa's a time for African-Americans to think about our culture and our history and our community. We celebrate it from December 26 through January 1 with dancing and art and food and family."

Janie thought for a moment. "You know, we have different traditions, but it sounds like we all celebrate hope, caring, family and giving back. Sure we have presents and trees and Santa Claus, but Christmas is about peace on Earth, goodwill and hope."

Elizabeth Chapin-Pinotti

"Maybe our celebration should be about hope and doing nice things for people," said Jessi.

"That would be awesome," Aadab added. "The reason for our season – good deeds and peace together."

"We could call it Kwanmisadomakuh," Janie said.

"I love it!" said Naomi. "Kwanmisadomakuh it is."

"Let's go tell Mrs. Banks," Jessi said excited about the prospect.

"Let's choose purple and blue as our colors," Janie said.

"And we'll have treats from all of our different cultures and instead of gifts or a big party, we'll do something nice for the needy."

"Like the kids in the cancer center – who have to stay there all the time," Janie was excited too.

"And the homeless, we have to help the homeless," Jessi said.

"Let's collect socks and warm clothes," Aadab added.

Mrs. Banks loved the idea.

The very next day, they were in small groups and discussing holidays they'd chosen out of a hat researching when Little Wolf approached Janie and her friends. Little Wolf's first name was Mike, his middle name was Little Wolf. He liked Little Wolf better thank Mike.

As soon as he cleared his throat and she looked at his sad eyes – it hit her. She forgot him!

"Everyone is always forgetting us," Little Wolf said, "I never thought you would too. You come to Big Time. You watch us dance."

Janie boinked her head with her hand. "Oh man! I am so sorry! I just…"

"Everyone always justs…"he said, but Mrs. Banks interrupted.

"I didn't forget Little Wolf," she said. "We're starting here with Big Time and then we will have a day of studying Ramadan and Christmas and many other holidays."

Little Wolf smiled. "Good because I like our new holiday. I want hope and peace too!"

At Rockville Elementary School that December, the children sang songs about hope, they wrote letters to soldiers in the military, they gathered food for the hungry, they visited the elderly in nursing homes, they made cards and books for the children in the hospital and they gathered and gave away socks and warm clothes.

Everyone joined in and the spirit of the holiday season was alive and well in the hope and good deeds of Kwanmisadomakuh.

On December 24, Janie told her entire family about the December celebration she and her class made up. She told them how they learned about each holiday but focused on hope and spreading kindness.

"Janie," Nono said as he cut the prime rib, "you and your friends may be on to something, because, after all, that is what the season is truly about – no matter what you believe."

"We all just wanted to give a little hope for the future – peace on earth and warm socks to all," Janie said.

They raised their Christmas glasses and cheered: "Here's to peace on earth and warm socks to all."

They all clinked their glasses.

Kwanmisadomakuh Big Time!

Comprehension Quiz

1. Janie jumps out of bed and is excited because···
   a) It is Thanksgiving
   b) It is Christmas
   c) It is December 1
   d) It is December 25

2. Mother tells Janie that they may not celebrate Christmas in her classroom. What is the reason?
   a) It is July
   b) It is a public school
   c) It is a Catholic school
   d) Janie is quitting school

3. The four holidays or celebrations mentioned in the story are:
   a) Ramadan, Hanukkah, Christmas and Big Time
   b) Ramadan, Easter, July 4th and Halloween
   c) Ramadan, Hanukkah, Christmas and Thanksgiving
   d) Ramadan, Hanukkah, Christmas and New Year's Day

4. What holiday does Janie's friend Naomi celebrate in December
   a) Christmas
   b) Ramadan
   c) Big Time
   d) Hanukkah

5. What holiday is celebrated by fasting?
   a) Christmas
   b) Ramadan
   c) Big Time
   d) Hanukkah

6. What festival is celebrated during Big Time?
   a) Oktoberfest
   b) Acorn
   c) Corn
   d) Half Moon

7. What does the new holiday Janie and her friends created center around?
   a) Hope and peace
   b) The Festival of Lights
   c) Harvest
   d) New Year's Day

#2

Kwanmisadomakuh Big Time!

Problem:

_____

_____

_____

_____

Solution:

_____

_____

_____

_____

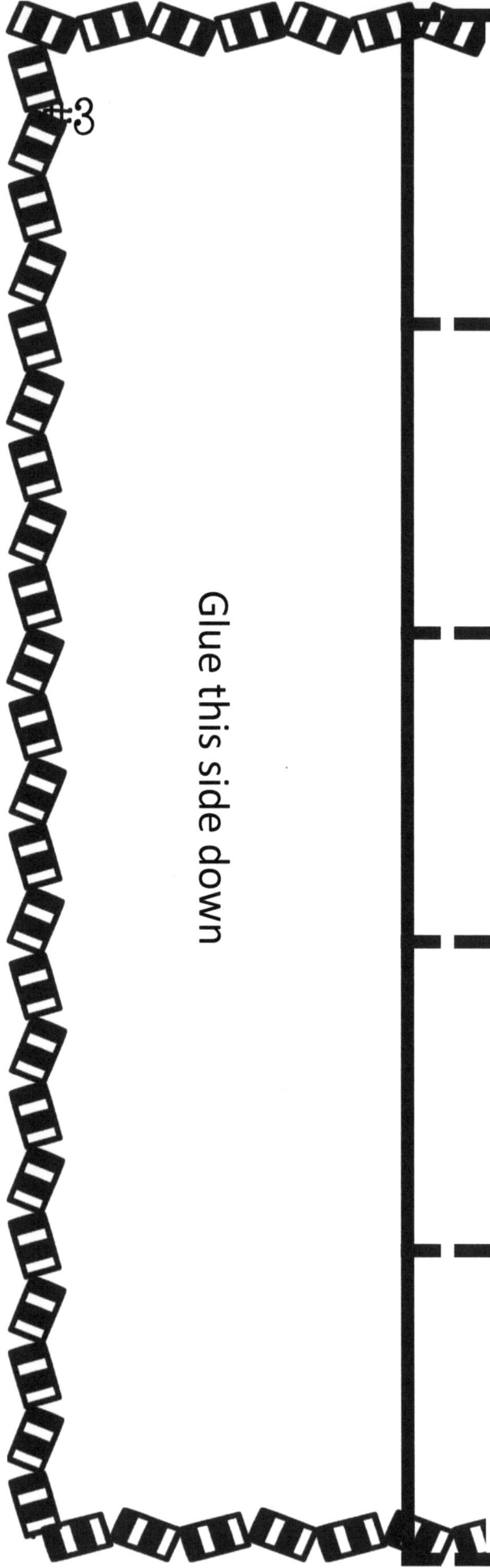

#3

Glue this side down

Three Words to
Describe Janie

Three Words to
Describe Aadab

Three Words to
Describe Jessi

Three Words to
Describe Naomi

Three Words to
Describe Little Wolf

Cut along the dots.

About Kwanmisadomakuh #4

What is your favorite part of the story? _____
_____

Details why…
1. _____

_____

2. _____

_____

Who is your favorite character? _____
_____

Details why…
1. _____

_____

2. _____

_____

What is the main problem or conflict in the story? _____
_____

Details…
1. _____

_____

2. _____

_____

Summarize Kwanmisadomakuh Big Time!

In the beginning...

After that...

Later...

Just when...

At the end...

In the beginning _____

_____

_____

_____

After that _____

_____

_____

_____

_____

Later _____

_____

_____

_____

_____

Just when _____

_____

_____

_____

_____

At the end _____

_____

_____

_____

_____

Glue this to your notebook.

Motivation and Evidence

What is Janie's Motivation

Plus...

Evidence to Support My Thoughts

What are Janie's Friends Motivation

Plus...

Evidence to Support My Thoughts

What is Little Wolf's Motivation

Plus...

Evidence to Support My Thoughts

Name: _____

Stop and Think #7

Little Wolf and Big Time seem like afterthoughts to the story but they were specifically placed to be symbolic. What do you think their position in the story symbolizes?

_____
_____
_____
_____
_____
_____
_____
_____
_____
_____
_____
_____
_____
_____
_____
_____
_____

Why is this story important to American today? _____

_____
_____
_____
_____
_____
_____
_____

Stop and Think #7 – General Ideas

Little Wolf and Big Time seem like afterthoughts to the story but they were specifically placed to be symbolic. What do you think their position in the story symbolizes?

Through much of United States history Native Americans have been treated like non-entities or, worse yet, animals. They've been pushed out of their land, overlooked and have even had bounties placed on their "hides". The "hey wait!" is symbolic of how easy it is for us, even today, with historical knowledge, to overlook the importance of Native Americans and their holidays, separate from those "traditionally" deriving from the European Colonial collective history.

In a broader sense, the almost afterthought of the Big Time addition is symbolic of how people often, inadvertently think what they believe or celebrate is the only way or the right way to celebrate. While differences are easy to overlook – we must mindfully be culturally inclusive and respective to everyone. After all, our differences, culturally and individually, are part of what makes things interesting.

Why is this story important to American today? This story is important to America today because our country is diverse and it is important to be respectful of everyone and everyone's differences.

www.ingramcontent.com/pod-product-compliance
Lightning Source LLC
Chambersburg PA
CBHW041545040426
42447CB00002B/54